ANIMAL TAG TEAMS

Nile Crocodiles and Egyptian Plovers

by Kari Schuetz

BLASTOFF! READERS 3

BELLWETHER MEDIA • MINNEAPOLIS, MN

Note to Librarians, Teachers, and Parents:

Blastoff! Readers are carefully developed by literacy experts and combine standards-based content with developmentally appropriate text.

Level 1 provides the most support through repetition of high-frequency words, light text, predictable sentence patterns, and strong visual support.

Level 2 offers early readers a bit more challenge through varied simple sentences, increased text load, and less repetition of high-frequency words.

Level 3 advances early-fluent readers toward fluency through increased text and concept load, less reliance on visuals, longer sentences, and more literary language.

Level 4 builds reading stamina by providing more text per page, increased use of punctuation, greater variation in sentence patterns, and increasingly challenging vocabulary.

Level 5 encourages children to move from "learning to read" to "reading to learn" by providing even more text, varied writing styles, and less familiar topics.

Whichever book is right for your reader, Blastoff! Readers are the perfect books to build confidence and encourage a love of reading that will last a lifetime!

This edition first published in 2019 by Bellwether Media, Inc.

No part of this publication may be reproduced in whole or in part without written permission of the publisher. For information regarding permission, write to Bellwether Media, Inc., Attention: Permissions Department, 6012 Blue Circle Drive, Minnetonka, MN 55343.

Library of Congress Cataloging-in-Publication Data

Names: Schuetz, Kari, author.
Title: Nile Crocodiles and Egyptian Plovers / by Kari Schuetz.
Description: Minneapolis, MN : Bellwether Media, Inc., [2019] | Series: Blastoff! Readers. Animal Tag Teams | Audience: Ages 5-8. | Audience: K to grade 3. | Includes bibliographical references and index.
Identifiers: LCCN 2018033937 (print) | LCCN 2018034673 (ebook) | ISBN 9781681036861 (ebook) | ISBN 9781626179561 (hardcover : alk. paper)
Subjects: LCSH: Mutualism (Biology)–Juvenile literature. | Nile crocodile–Behavior–Juvenile literature. | Pluvianus aegyptius–Behavior–Juvenile literature. | Plovers–Behavior–Juvenile literature.
Classification: LCC QH548.3 (ebook) | LCC QH548.3 .S38 2019 (print) | DDC 577.8/52–dc23
LC record available at https://lccn.loc.gov/2018033937

Editor: Betsy Rathburn   Designer: Brittany McIntosh

Printed in the United States of America, North Mankato, MN

Table of Contents

A Tooth Cleaning

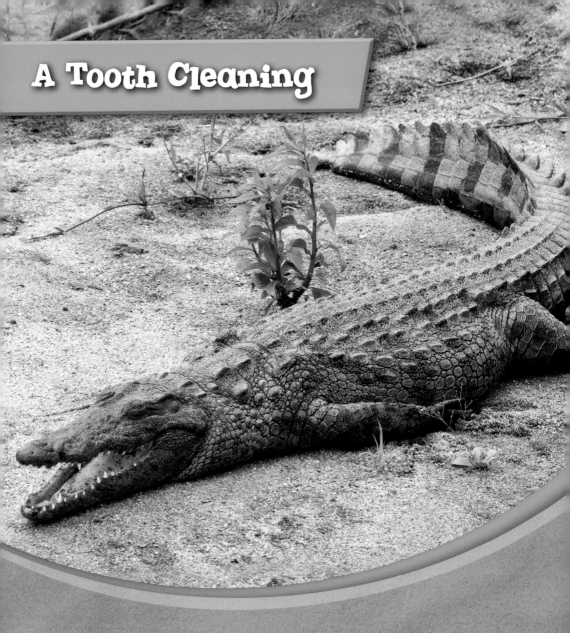

A Nile crocodile suns itself on a riverbank. It holds its mouth wide open.

Soon, an Egyptian plover comes over. The bird eats food stuck between the crocodile's teeth!

Nile crocodiles and Egyptian plovers share a **habitat** south of the Sahara **Desert** in Africa.

Tag Team Range

= Nile crocodile and Egyptian plover range

The animals can be found together in rivers and **wetlands**. These friendly neighbors display **symbiosis**. They help one another!

Nile crocodiles are some of the largest **reptiles** alive. They have long, flat bodies covered in scales.

Their V-shaped heads hold strong, toothy jaws. Many of their teeth stick out at all times.

Nile Crocodile Profile

type: reptile
length: 20 feet (6 meters)
weight: up to 2,200 pounds (1,000 kilograms)
life span: up to 80 years

The crocodiles often
stay hidden underwater.
Only their eyes and
nostrils show.

nostril

These **carnivores** wait for fish, birds, and other **prey** to come close. Then, they attack by surprise!

Egyptian plovers are small birds with short, strong beaks. Most of their feathers are black, white, and gray.

Black feathers on their faces look like masks. But the feathers on their bellies are orange!

Egyptian Plover Profile

type: **bird**
length: **8 inches (20 centimeters)**
weight: **around 3 ounces (85 grams)**
life span: **unknown**

The plovers stand and move on long, thin legs. These **omnivores** often **wade** along shores to feed.

wading

They dig for and peck at **insects**, worms, and seeds.

Helping Each Other

Nile crocodiles usually try to eat birds. However, these **predators** do not chomp at Egyptian plovers. They let the plovers sit on them.

The birds eat up
annoying **parasites**!

Plovers offer dental care to crocodiles, too. They feed on food bits jammed between the crocodiles' teeth.

The birds may also warn the crocodiles of danger. They call out when predators are near. Then, they fly to safety.

Nile crocodiles and Egyptian plovers team up to keep one another healthy.

Tag Team Trades

Nile crocodiles

provide meals

Egyptian plovers

clean teeth

eat pests

The crocodiles offer a food source.
The birds offer a cleaning service.
This trade helps both animals survive!

Glossary

carnivores—animals that only eat meat

desert—an area of land that gets little rain

habitat—the natural environment where a plant or animal lives

insects—small, six-legged animals that have bodies divided into three parts

nostrils—openings through which an animal breathes

omnivores—animals that eat both meat and plants

parasites—living things that use other living things to survive; parasites harm their hosts.

predators—animals that hunt other animals for food

prey—animals that are hunted by other animals for food

reptiles—cold-blooded animals that have bony plates or scales and breathe air

symbiosis—a close relationship between very different living things

wade—to walk through water that is not very deep

wetlands—land areas that have wet soil; swamps and marshes are wetlands.

To Learn More

AT THE LIBRARY

Jenkins, Steve, and Robin Page. *How to Clean a Hippopotamus: A Look at Unusual Animal Partnerships.* Boston, Mass.: Houghton Mifflin Books for Children, 2010.

Miller, John. *Winston & George*. New York, N.Y.: Enchanted Lion Books, 2014.

Zayarny, Jack. *Symbiosis*. New York, N.Y.: Smartbook Media, Inc., 2017.

ON THE WEB

FACTSURFER

Factsurfer.com gives you a safe, fun way to find more information.

1. Go to www.factsurfer.com.

2. Enter "Nile crocodiles and Egyptian plovers" into the search box.

3. Click the "Surf" button and select your book cover to see a list of related web sites.

Index

The images in this book are reproduced through the courtesy of: Alexander Cher, front cover (crocodile); Sue Robinson, front cover (plover), pp. 6-7 (plover), 13, 16 (plover); Bob Gibbons/ Alamy, p. 4; Warren Photography, p. 5; Papilio/ Alamy, pp. 6-7 (crocodile); dioch, p. 8; Benny Marty, p. 9; Utopia_88, pp. 10, 11; Manakin, p. 12; AGAMI Photo Agency/ Alamy, p. 14; Robert HENNO/ Alamy, p. 15; Chris Kruger, p. 16 (crocodile); Martin Mecnarowski, p. 16 (crocodile); Oliver Smart/ Alamy, p. 17 (plovers); Juniors Bildarchiv GmbH/ Alamy, p. 18; Clayton Burne, pp. 19, 21 (right); Volodymyr Burdiak, p. 20 (left); Janelle Lugge, p. 21 (crocodile); NHPA/ SuperStock, p. 21 (plover).